T0065196

AuthorHouse™
1663 Liberty Drive
Bloomington, IN 47403
www.authorhouse.com
Phone: 833-262-8899

Published by AuthorHouse   04/04/2023

ISBN: 978-1-6655-5539-5 (sc)
ISBN: 978-1-6655-5538-8 (e)

Writing
Calms

J.S. CHRISTIAN

authorHOUSE®

Contents

Pray-gerism

I must first confess to you

none of these works are mine.

Credit goes to the Creator;

The Genesis far more divine.

I pray-gerized every verse.

Inspired by the call

God is the real author and

the finisher of all

Fighting Psalms

Divine inspired messengers embattle
when trying to disseminate
His words

Flagrant noises are
Petulantly Fighting
Psalmists in their efforts
to be heard

This is how I picture it
A palm against my forehead
An arm outstretched
A bridge between us formed

I'm flailing kicking swinging

Screaming

Leaning in

Judged valiant seeing

Warriors fighting

tackling the storm

Not falling
Palm is steadying
Not failing
Prayer is readying

No stopping

stinging singing swarming

Wrongs

Prayer Psalms for
Songs uniting
Hit the last note
Halt dividing

The inspiration

writing

fighting PSALMS

Thee Scriber

Thee Scriber is humble kissed
Picked. Did not apply for this
Or study days for ways to prophesy

Weighted by prophetic words
Uplifted by the message heard
Then written
As inspired; guided by

Chronicled when put upon
The highest compensation comes
From higher places. Never earthly from
Thee Scriber still with breath is never done.

The last man

standing

is the true victor

only if he stands

for Good

No One

I've never known someone of None.
Created from themselves
Conceived from own seed planted, rooted
grown from
No One else.
Yet here we are
Adrift
Afar
Aloft
Alone
Astray

No one's
Some of
Someone's son

Detached then gone astray

Please take the time

To read my mind.

Beckon me back to pray

Omnipresently

When we decide to change how we see

D

O

G

How everything looks will change.

G.ood O.le D.ays

Ah, the Good Old Days!
Everything was nice

All the people, places
Neighborhoods
Kind and so polite!

The Good Old Days
Were pleasant
Folks were friendly
Most were kind

We saw who and when
we wanted
Those we didn't
Didn't mind

Grownups were in charge of kids
Children couldn't 'cuss'
Honoring our G.O.D.
This way for all of us

Although we may look different,
the message is the same
Good old days live forever
Within context of His name

Ah, G.O.D. on speed dial
A wondrous glorious way
To keep the good old days
Alive each and every way

G.O.D. connections vary
in how each receives

God

Omnipresently
For those who believe

Hearing

On knees, wheeled seats
or standing
God knows and listens
to our hearts
Hears when we pray
paths future days
then never departs

Rock Solid

I have been trying
to slip out a while
God keeps on
blocking the door

Just when I think
I have reached
the rock bottom

He says,
"Rest,
that's my rock on the floor!"

Neither mud nor it quicksand
It is solid
bears weight

Of your burdens,
your debts
Every single heartache

And your children?
I've got them.
No cause for alarm.

I too hold them
tightly
with you in my arms.

So stand up my daughter!

Stand strong my son!

Rock bottom is still
my rock
you're standing on

Palliative

Remove the thorn from lion's paw.
Hold a trembling hand.

Give a child a warm embrace.
Help them to understand.

The world is big and frightening.
We live until we die.

Sometimes we laugh til our bellies ache.
Some aching makes us cry.

God promises us palliative love.
Embracing Him through pain.

Never alone en route to home
Until we dance again

Pinto

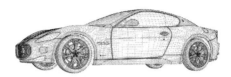

It's tough selling Maseratis
driving Pintos

Hard to train for marathons
from the couch

Tough to criticize another person's posture

Without addressing just how very much you slouch

Cheerleaders smirking grumbled fight songs

With frowns and mumbles motivate no one

Try smiling on the inside first
happiness habits when rehearsed

This is how the best cheering is done

Show Son shine lives within you
joy divinely binds

Show yourself then everyone else
The link to real good times!

Truth steps forward

when standing

toe to toe

with lies

Mycroscope

Its clear you have looked
Into me
I am dying
To see all you can see
As you are
Poking. Peeking.
Down inside.

My mind?

Is it smart enough?

My heart?

Too kind or
Kinda rough?

Any evidence of all the times
I cried
(Out to you)

My life examined
Does it pass?
Exude good character and class

Relay now

what your microscope
reveals

At a glance,
any chance

my heart can heal?

One Day

One day

correct will not be political

Right

Will be one direction

Left

Will be the other way

They will join at intersections

Children will all be childish

Distinguishable

From adults

Resolution will most matter

Not shaming those at fault

Worth will not be determined

By sight, only by deed

Fair honest ways

Will be conveyed

One day

One day

One day

I say

Lord, can we please?

Okay One Day

Sometimes it's OK
To not be
OK
It's acceptable
not to be fine.
To need just
a minute
To not
be with it.
To want
just a little
more time...

So; when see me
I am looking down
Not speaking yet thinking
Grateful to be found

Not right now
Soon maybe
I will be one day
With fervent prayer
En route to
OKAY

Hang On!

Hang on little brother there's
always something else to do

This is temporary.
You are permanently you.

Together you and I will make it through!

So hang on little brother.
Just reach up and grab my hand.

Know that God would never give you
more than you could stand.

Remember your best yesterday.
Go visit in your mind.
See this as the day before then
Plan to have a real good time

(Together you and I will make it through!)

Lay it down! Don't hesitate;
mind and body deep in prayer.

Yeah, it's manly crying out.
You're not the only soul in there.

Whether alone and silent
aloud hidden in the crowd.
There is always
something else to do.

Yes, your God and my God will pull us through

Enough

I love you enough to hold you
Accountable for the fact I do
Feel
Responsible for loving you
Still
Close enough to
Fold
Tight enough to
Hold
breath blended
with my own
Inhaling
Enough
so when the last is left

Wailing
Oh, the wailing

I'm still
real

deep enough inside
you holding me
Beside

Enough

Poetry requires readers to breathe

Without readers
Poetry has no pulse

Context

Love is a word overused.
Underfelt

Love should never be abused
Wept

Love is a four letter word.
Profane

Love is of the sound mind
Insane

Love is oft misunderstood
Mistook

Love is often unrequited
Overlooked

Love is elementary
Believe

Love is epistemological
Breathe

Love is for people only;
all people love like...

People.

Love people. LOVE PEOPLE.
Alright?

Endearing Endurance

Dear Lord

Know that we are
thankful for
Your Son, the sun,
Faith to endure.
One team of
Difference;
Blessed same.
United in your
Holy name

Dear Langston,

Purveyor of poetry, you asked Me, what happens when dreams are deferred?

Well, they never wake, for deference sake.
Slumber seems the dream venue preferred.

They mushroom in darkness. They grow
through the night.
Not festering;
Awaiting...
the kiss of sunlight.

Why did you pose question prophetically?
Just say it. Is there something inside you
can see?

Love,
Me

Just In Case

JUST IN CASE
They can't play basketball.
Or run fast
Around the track at all.
Or sing and dance
Let's take a chance.
And educate our kids.

JUST IN CASE
A chase to catch
Falls short
Of the scouter' s match for any sport.
Let's academically work out.
And educate our kids.

When math and science
clearly seem.
The best recruiter and best team

Let's shift implicit bias back
Include all students
And all facts
Please EDUCATE ALL KIDS

We Po'

Me and Edgar Allan
Poe

Pour hearts out
in the words

Placed in our minds
So all can find

Inspiration heard
Me, Edger Allen,
Poe
Riches come from
prose

A wealth of verse
Exhumed, rehearsed
Poetry
Juxtaposed

Rewards?
They come in
Heaven
Countless artists
Know

Frugal fame
Fraternity
Me,
Edger Allen,
po'

Veterans Pray

Thank you, Lord
for this
Day and
Everything
it brings my way
and
Thank you for a
Voice to Pray
You'll guide my thoughts
and what I say
As I listen and obey.

Penultimate

Yesterday

The last speech was the next to last
time leaders had to say:

"Thoughts and prayers for the lives
of service members lost today"

When you make the promise
keep it
So will not need
Repeat it
Then relay

Condolences so kind
Folded flags, held to remind
of the honor and the sacrifices made
So the next to last goodbye is
not in vain.
Lord make the last goodbyes
the ones we do

Today.

R.I.P.

There's unraveling hatred
pulling apart
the U.S. seams' holding duration

May they R.ot I.n P.eril
tools used
To chisel binding ties of this nation

For centuries so taut contriving
divisions betwixt became blurred
Covered up by the dust of scampering footsteps.
Flags unfurled.

across state lines shifting timelines to and fro.
Bros.

R.est I.n P.raise the souls of author
introspection who wrote

The battle messages concisely
crafted, timely shared

For all times first inside then outside blared

Rote repleting worth repeating oft to strike a chord

Rhythmic orders moving armies honor forward

defeated tools and weapons dared

Used against Almighty armament; HA so HA!
Aware

(though no humor thinking hate so close to vic'try
R.est I.n P.rayer.)

(season)

All of us were created

for a reason.

For a cause.

With speaking voices

For our season

To praise

Praiseworthy things

To celebrate

Unite

To sing

Psalms from inspiration

the Creator brings

TREE Fell Silent

If a TREE falls in the forest
With no one there to listen

Does the TREE even make a sound?

No SHE does not.

No one is around.

Willing to hear the yelling
Or the felling
To the ground

From the brown TREE
toppled over

Broken
Cracked

All splintered out

Ugly crying
Other trees denying

Hearing the TREE shout

In the forest there; not for us
Sounds suppress
Swallowed reliance

Conservation
Needed for the Strength
Of next felling in silence

Invisible everywhere
Praying to be found

S.ad
H.earts
E. cho

God always hears the sounds

When our own brothers stand against us

Who are the ones to truly blame?

Those who dare divide our blood

Or Blood who dare smear it on our name?

VENEER

Yes, of course
I can leap
your tall buildings

Blindfolded,
straight parallel park

Pinky finger
grappling hook climb

Up steep mountain sides
in the dark

Keep it all together
Straddling Seismic Fault Lines
for miles

**I just need a hand
with my smile**

Truth Is

We are better when we decide to work together
As a nation 50 strategies won't do
We cannot devise deciding on
seceding

Based on parties, based on margins, based on hues
The very name of us would have to be dissected
Weakened by corrosive strife and constant hate

America, get it together.
Now or sooner
Try-to-be-better

Before we fall apart
or it is too late

Truth is the U.S. flag still flies high for one nation
Creatives build on rights to say the varied same
In different colors, different causes, varied accents

U.S.A.
is still united in His name.

True Sayings

Truths are only ugly to liars
Victimless crime is an oxymoron
Things you cannot see
are everywhere
You can only take a stand on ground you're on

You cannot complain if you are able to complain
Praise each meal your last was not your last
Time moves too slow when you are waiting
When someone waits for you, times moves too fast

There is only so much you can hide in closets
There is only so much space on every shelf
God, acknowledged, smiles when you finally admit
"I cannot do this all by myself!"

Love Returns

Try to LOVE
Before
It leaves you

Try to live
Before you die

Try to store more
Memories
Of moments

You laughed so hard
You cried

Overflow the fun
Deposit box
With silliness and smiles

Then just keep them up
Way up
in there awhile

Sit back and watch how
Much they grow

The love thoughts
On their own

Don't forget to add
your favorite song
(dance when it comes on!)

Visit this place on days
You feel like
You are all alone

Love Returns grow so
Invest.Know.
His love is never gone

roots of deception

should remain

under trampled

grounds

Real

I don't slip into this skin by day
Take it off at night
Pretend to be your friend;
And grin
To help you seem polite

I'm not wearing latest bodysuit
Yes, color is in style

Dermatologically
It's me!
And I refuse to smile

At night so you can
See me –ha!
Joke got old when
It was new

Will not sing or dance
Partake parlance
Though I will
pray with you

And I will pray for you!

Playbook

If you win then what?

Then what

If you win then what?

You made a play
Then took a stand

Though how will vict'ry look?

Hold up a picture.
Share your plan

Your template
Your main diagram

Who's left standing in the end?
Who gave?
Who took?

Real Winners
follow
His instructions
Book.

Know game is over
In the end
When better bigger
Hearted win

All break then shake
To play again.
Befriend

Used Hearts

New ones have the
new love smell

More smiles
Less miles

Can handle well

The virgin first rides
round love lanes carefree

Going down hills way too fast

All gain
No pain

Forevers last

Foresee.

Tons of fun and
I love you's

This will always be
So true

Suspensions tensions
Tenseness are all new

Used ones cost less

The breaks have worn

with more miles on them
Dings are from

bumpy places
potholes puddles pangs

In and out for shock repair

Dents and scratches
Everywhere

Never quite right
Somethings always wrong

Often used

More often worn

Never sure where damage from

Costs less to get.
More ample lot
To choose.

Know Higher covers for
Used hearts
(love truths)

Real Men

Real men encourage their kids
Follow through as biggest fans
Appreciate real women
Make requests. Never demands.

Real men 'hit on' women
(just on)
With no real contact
Save the fury for the boxing ring
The gym
The field and track

Have a soft spot for their mothers
Try to walk on Father's way
Know it's manly when men fear God
Are not ashamed to pray

For neighbors, country, world peace.
For selves; eternal life.
The world needs more real men

Signed, a Real man's wife

V·O·T·E

When we pray then….

V. oice
O. ur
T. houghts
E. lectorally

It's then and how we are heard.
Put your fingerprint on history.
Is Electorally even a word?

Just Believe...

God knows

AND

loves

you

(unconditionally)

Imagine that!

Good Guy

He is not God
so why the
trembling?
He is not God
so why the
fear?

He's just a man
who has no plan to hurt you.

He's huge, that's true
Though so are you

With what it is you

Plan to do
To hurt him.

When you call to cause alarm

See your father
See your son

See our Father and His son

See a man there who has...

No plans to hurt you.

Winning Minds

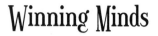

When intellect contradicts melanin content;

B.S. Oxymoron. Oh my!

If a few are let in
then supremacy ends

And equality may go awry.
Man your stations, coasts, schools, and your status!
Scholars rise above blocked
walls and gates

Armed with the Almighty's Handbook of Highering.

Winning! Pitting love against hate.

Mathematic Solution

Hate times hate
Is hate squared
Times one more hate
It's cubed

Multiplied
It replicates
Regurgitates
Renewed

Hate added
Just reflects itself
Division
Does the same

Subtracting
Is the only way
That hate
Can be contained

Bore With Me

Boredom Day is coming!
imagine if there was nothing to disagree over;
fight, or argue about
Be ashamed for, envy. Hate.

How boring.

Lord, please move us to
this time long overdue
so we can
Cheerfully
"Save the Date"

Everything

When you try to take
My everything
That matters most to me

I see what of me
Matters
Most to you

These things of your
Obsession
My everythings
Are not possessions

To remove

How can I help you
Help yourself
To move along
Be someone else

Help you to seek and
Find
A modicum of
TRUTH

My everything
I willful share
There's room
For all

Everywhere!

And for everyone
No need to soul
Remove

No need to sneak.
My everything
Is within reach
And hovering

If want to
take some
Of my Everything
Please do

For Heaven's sake
There's enough
Everything.

It's Truth

Adult Tree

Cherry trees have cherries
Peach trees bear their name

Apple trees content vary
Fig trees mostly look the same

They all begin as saplings
Grow into something sweet

All good with temping goodness
All except the Adult Tree.

It is pretty. It grows poisonous.
It has Branches. It grows vines.

Adult Tree first bites seem delicious
Whither insides over time

So have a peach, cherry or apple
Folded warm inside a pie

A much sweeter post repentance
Can't deny

Precision

When you take the time
to do it
Take enough to
Do it right

If you get it right
the first time
You won't
Have to do it twice

So no matter what the
IT is
Clear concise and careful
Plans

Provide the path
Make concise math to
do it right
Again

And again

Preventive Cares

Since…

1. Ironically illegal
2. Chance of fail
3. Illogical irrational
4. BFF wails
5. Lose due rights
6. Kids could see
7. There's tomorrow
8. Your legacy
9. Call incoming from above
10. You undoing
11. Insult love
12. Insult family
13. Will look odd
14. Deny Heaven
15. Piss of God
16. Deny success for foolish fleeing
17. Breathing
18. Seeing
19. Hearing
20. Being
21. Many good things left to do
22. Music
23. Brownies
24. Ice Cream too!

25. Brilliant sunsets
26. Awesome son
27. Walks to take
28. Paths to run
29. Your Country
30. Blessings count
31. Wealth shared in varied amounts
32. Games to play
33. Games to win
34. Present presents
35. Future friends
36. Doctors
37. Feel. Good.
38. Humor
39. Laughs
40. Clearly straight and narrow paths
41. Tell-a-vision
42. Selfishness
43. Your Mom
44. Your Dad
45. Erase goodness
46. Reduced to number
47. Go to hell
48. Effing stranger; story tells
49. Whole world sad
50. No way to hide

at least 50 reasons why NOT to suicide. think
of going long enough, will get your wish one
day. Not immortal; may be 50 years away.

Heirborne

I'm not jumping without a parachute
Or power rockets on my boots
No matter how effing sad I am

Borne. I already aced the test
My beating heart, my breath – SUCCESS!
Even when nobody gives a dayum

Though...
If I forget, can't handle it and
try to quit by winging it
Or make a choice to go out on a limb

Or, out of cash, I dash to splash.
I pray I can remember that
I'm Heir borne

Thank God that I can swim

Born

Beautiful priceless
Diamond
and the source from
whence it comes

Are both vital
In their own way

Both aware of
Where they're from

The beauty outcomes
Shine through darkness
One will glisten
Source unseen

Creates pressure
Formed a jewel
Adored
For all eternity

Waterways

When I drink the water
I do not analyze the elements
I'm dry and water's wet
To quench my thirst

Can't taste 2
hydrogen
Hydrations

One oxygen
Oxygenated

Only recalling that the parching
was there first

Likewise a spirit
Can get dried out
Fears and tears all
Can get cried out

Earthly elements can offer
Only grief

So choose to take it
Higher
Drink the word to
douse the fire

Cool the flames with
Holy Waters of belief.

Plenty

There is enough for everyone.

There is enough love
Enough fairness
Enough laughter

To share with

Enough caring to give some to to everyone
Enough to keep bearing the weight of too much fun

Enough joy for smiles
Though far too many frowns

God promises enough to go around

Quint-Tree-Central

The 5th tree behind
the other four
took just as long to grow
it's just as tall
it's just as thick

Yet other arbors steal the show

The first tree is most visible.
The second gets the breeze.
Tree three can feel
sun glimmers still.
The fourth is within reach.

The fifth is nature's humble fort
stands strong and iou
layers in rings.

Holds blue jays in the wind, sways, as the robins perch
to sing.

the fifth's the quintessential
of asking for nothing more
than to be
the only tree

obscured divine
yet clandestine adored.

Insider

When you live inside
Whale's belly,
You see
Wha
Whe

Who
He eats

Just prior to digested self
once a delicious treat

Take lessons from the blessing of
the redemptive glance

With a whale of revelation
from the second chance

High Noon

I'll bring a rose to your gun fight

So we have to stand at close range

To see Eye 2 Eye

Hoping both can rely

On minds motives and

Moves making change.

Since I'm packing a rose,

please bring water

Since you're packing a gun,

I'll bring pleas

To stand foes–future–friends

Locked and loaded to end

Understanding the

Victor is

PEACE.

Simply

Like things
Love people
All people

Love people who like things
Even if they are different

Things

Like people.

Who they love

Wood And Jesus

Looking up at wood and Jesus
No expression on my face
This is the hour you can
Count me out
See me adorned in grace

Three dots one 6 seconds prior
The fire inside me will still burn
For fervent prayer
Peace and
Compassion
Understanding
Lessons learn

I may seem down because
I'm lying down
Not out
Or indisposed

Neither downtrodden

Nor forgotten
Quiet.
Finally reposed

Nothing new,
The wood and Jesus.
Standing, looked up
Through and through

Lying down
In wood with
Jesus.

Pray I am looking
Down at you.

Designated Driver

He had so many
Rejections and
Failures
In his life

With college
With career
With battling
Strife

Ending it all
Just seemed
To make
More sense

Though what
Baffled him most
He just couldn't ignore
Was the try-again-drive
was intense

"But why me; the stumbles?
Then why not me;
the jumper?"

The cliffhanger was

Why still alive?

(easy)
There are times we are
just designated to know
God is designated
to drive

Negate Hate

Negate hate with love
Negate ignorance with
learning

Knowing peace of understanding
Is what all should be yearning

Pet Peeves

Proudly looking

Over the mess

he planned and

ran to evil do

Styrofoam blood

from teddy bear

Wicked agenda

For those shoes

Denied (yea Lied) he knew of it
Then hung his head in shame

Claimed the cat and gerbil
did it
Causing discord with the blame

Seven!
Committed all
Of them
Promise
Never do it again!

Thank God
Pets aren't
accountable
Like us humans
when they sin.

I can clearly recall

disrespecting my parents only once.

Transgressions after then

were all blurry.

Divine Limitations

Sure, there's…

The earth

The moon

The stars

The seas

The trees

And bees

The sun

Oceans and all in between.

Impressive work God's done.

His only limitation seems

He can't leave me alone!

Open Arms

Open arms
Can receive far more
than closed ones straddled

Open hearts
Can feel more love
than hardened ones embattled

Open minds
Can hold more ideas
and gain far more knowledge

Open schools
Can send more children
Educated off to college

To open doors
And hearts
And minds

Of closed ones;
The very same

Then walk through those doors together
Opened honoring His name

APB

Put out an

All Points Bulletin

For those suspects who

Come packing their ambitions

And full entitlements to ...

a home, good education, domestic

tranquility,

rights to happiness, due process, life and

liberty,

and any church of worship.

With or without seating.

Put out an APB for

All People Breathing

Higher Construct

We hold these truths of having
Been created equal tightly

In so doing, we remind ourselves in prayer
daily and nightly

Focus on goodness, self rely
Self sustain, boldly cry

Be true to who and how God made you stand

Educate where lessons come
Never hold out flattened palms
To beg
Instead rotate to shake a hand

(Your brothers hand)

Only look down
To tie your shoes and to teach young
Children who

Look up to you
As good women
And men

Seek favor only from above
Love all people. Receive love.
Again.

United States of America

United

        means together bound

States

        are the mosaics found

Of

        is the belonging to

America

        is me and you
        End United divisions games
        Or draft the docs to change
        the same

        (God prefers united all under His name)

Truth In Light

The truth: there was a lot of pain

He lost a lot of friends

He gained wealth of understanding of what

Matters in the end

Dialogues resonated
Looked inflated in his mind

"Why would you even go there
knowing they don't like your kind?"

Heard from them all –
the messengers, gate keepers,
pseudo friends

This IS my place.
I am here. KIND.
No longer can pretend

To not seem rude and ugly
Heavy TRUTH burden to bear

All good with LIGHT
Not alone
Taking it everywhere

Never been more beautiful
In life.

Never looked more beautiful
In LIGHT.

Thee Scriber

Thee Scriber is humble kissed
Picked. Did not apply for this
Or study days for ways to prophesy

Weighted by prophetic words
Uplifted by the message heard
Then written
As inspired; guided by

Chronicled when put upon
The highest compensation comes
From higher places. Never earthly from
Thee Scriber still with breath is never done.

Up!

I am sometimes unsure where
I am yet my faith keeps
growing. Always
most certain
Whose
I am.
Always
assured of
where I am going.
Grounded in the blessed
Promises.of. Thee.all. Knowing

1ST I LOVE YOU

When you say
"I love you."
What do the words from your mouth mean?
Are you mimicking some words you heard
In an 'I love you' routine?
If more time, would an ellipsis replace
the one dot after "you"
To allow more words
a greater depth
of what you feel is true?
Does simplicity relay what each
word expressed denotes
| (the subject)
Love (the verb)

You (that's me)

You wrote.

Is a much deeper connection hidden there within?

Or...

Period. Declaration. Hard stop.
I - to - You - The End?

Perhaps I'm overthinking this
Like first "I Love Yous" do

Trying too hard to pick apart.

Oh yea, I love you too!

The Living Constitution

The United States Constitution
was borne of the Living
Bible by thinking
Men.Alive
inspired to scribe

words as formed in the

Living constitution of all Times

N'Encore

| thought for
Heaven's
Sake
this just can't
be true

After what this
World
has all
already
been
through

Then | remember
clearly

World War one
then
World War two

Do you?

Noblesse Oblige

Our predecessors, Ancestors
Shed blood, sweat tears away

Cleared paths down roads to
Straight up;
Heal History today

We rode here on their shoulders
Will not trample on their backs

Or live down to expectations
Showing fool's view mocking tracts

Know we do not harbor hatred
Our ventricles are full

With life blood and love
For all mankind
Despite the pains they pulled

There are no retribution raids
Just around the bend

Rest assured what comes
your way
is not from our hands, friend

We have a Higher calling
All

Crown jewels now to don

A fate to live while loving then
Breathe Freely from
Now on

The faith to live while loving Him
Borne living Free
Now on!

Weightlifting

Weightless yet Heavy
this may be
the place for all.
ETERNITY

One day all blues
will only dwell in skies
the ills, the hurts, burdens
and bills
forgiving faults for living will
lighten life loads
for those who pray abide
Do Love. Give Kindness.

Hate Unload

share pains and grief

release untold

with Him who lifts the weight of how you roll

Behold

He spots you, guards from crushing worldly souls

BATON

I am a former Sprinter
Slowed down so running distances

Shortened distance, Marathoner,
so I walk.

Looking out for life trip hazards,
Stumbled over every one
until I settled down with Him to sit and talk

It is divine. It was divinity which yanked me
From the paths to nowhere fast I sped upon

Did nothing wrong except fall
short in reach extension
Reaching back now looking up with the baton

Regardless race, venue or pace,
I have to work out
Or move full weighted in transgression running slow

Put the past behind
Clear views of victory visions

Then move freely with contrition.

Behold!

Now I get it! Now with hands clenched interlocking
Sitting immobile. Holding Faith full exercised

Best fit to go because I know I am a Winner
Ready to launch, faithfully fixed upon the Prize.

STAYING HIGH

Mankind insists on flying
from all stations

varied heights

in every earthly way
they can

(then they have to land)

Faith holds the only
Death Defying
Perpetual High

Always uplifting to man

Amen

STAND?

When do I, also born 4th of July,
get a free state in America?
Have a stake in 'this
Land is our land'
with grace.
STAND
not cower
as planted shorn
overt disdain forlorn
subservient to the celebrated
Or abhor the Red.Wites witBlues?

Yeah

There are some happy people
There are some happy times
There are some good things

Happening

Where everything is fine

Heaven

I Would Choose You

If I could choose my friends and family

The cast would be the same

From taggers on
of who belongs to

ones who bear my name

These perfectly imperfects
just like me

Created to
Paint a life mosaic
As divinely chosen few
I will keep you

Every one of you

Even given a choice

You give volume and dimensions
To my voice

HIS BREAKTHROUGH

I did Catholicism easily
it taught me how to Guilt

And patience was a piece of cake
it's how Rome was built

The Great Wall of China –
easy climb
it was just a hill

Decathlons? Yeah bring em on!
Just 10 sports slots to fill

but success?
oh, what a mess!
a challenge
just a dream

I could not seem to master that

Now I know what it means

I went in and out and
Up and down

Then back to 'my place'

All because
I failed to see God's grace

I tried to do things my way
Looked in mirrors for a choice

The first time I heard
Victory!
Was when I heard His voice

Beckoned to the narrow path
Higher guidance how to steer

With peace of understanding as the breakthrough –
SUCCESS clear!

Sentence

Mom has to make it through her
sentence and his sentence

Without crying so that she
Can try explain

In time that's left
Her son is deaf
and trying signing
trying signing (not defying)

trying not dying!
when
the officer exclaims…

(She cries)

Dear Lord,
Please spell out
MERCY.

Translate for them Your grace

Share your voice
Block bitter noises

Bring
Hope, and Care,
and Faith

The Deaf Mute
pray
We can relay so
all will
Understand

Unhearing are denied
A voice
when someone binds their hands

Please And Thank You

I say "Please" when
crying out to Him

"Thank You" for work
He's done

Then "You're Welcome"
when I, in mass, revere
praise for only Son

Then 'Please' again
for mercy for my
Brothers gone astray

"Thank you" for listening
and this breath
You've given me today

"You're Welcome"
when I genuflect
(You catch me as I fall)

You are always Welcomed here
This being Your place and all.

Giveaway

There is no tax on kindness.

Delivery is fast and free

There is no hold time

Super long lines

It is a proven remedy

It cures hatred
Heartaches
Misery
It even stops race wars

Give away
Joy and Kindness
FREE!

What are you waiting for?

Wealth

Pray you are never too rich to accept kindness
Or too poor to not have some to spare

The giver and receiver both benefit from actions
Of growing gift of having just been there

So, for the sake of kindness,
Habituate giving blindly

So all can see
true wealth
you have to share
(-J-)

About the Book and Author

J.S. Christian writes in humble recognition
of the divine source of inspiration. The
recurring theme of advocating poetically was
borne of a penchant for conflict resolution
writing. Advocacy over protests. Civility over chaos.
Love over Hate. Humility. All for Goodness
sake.

"Advocate for our greatest natural resources;
people and peace"

Printed in the United States
by Baker & Taylor Publisher Services